MW00633508

10 things I wish I knew before I turned 18

To: my Beautiful Friend Carla

by: Kenneth Smith, Jr.

Copyright Page

All rights reserved. No parts of this publication may be reproduced, distributed, or transmitted in any form or by any means, including photocopying, recording, or other mechanical methods, without the prior written permission of the publisher, except in the case of brief quotations embodied in critical reviews and certain other noncommercial uses permitted by copyright law.

For permission requests, write to the publisher addressed: "Attention: Permissions Coordinator" and e-mail address below:

Gettingestablished3@gmail.com.

Ordering information

Quantity Sales – Special discounts are available in quantity purchases by corporations, associations, and networking groups. For details, contact Andrew Finch for Individual Sales.

ISBN-13: 978-0-9600163-0-3

Dedication

I dedicate this book to my future children in that you would know your dad is a hard worker and tries to live with purpose. Also, so that you would have a map to become a mature adult at a young age. I want you to be the best you can be, and I believe this book will help you.

Table of Contents

Foreword

By Derrick Butts: CEO AssistU2Win

I walk through life with a sense of purpose. My time is important and my connections are critical. I believe things don't happen just to happen. There is a divine that orchestrates life in such a way to cause paths to cross at certain moments in time. I have labeled these times as Intentional Intersections.

I was delivering a speech inside The Network Bar, a private members only bar I might add, and after the speech I noticed a young man and his Uncle (I found that out later) waiting around to speak to me. I shook both of their hands and began a conversation that intrigued me. The Uncle didn't say much, but you knew he cared for his nephew greatly to have accompanied him at this event. The young man with boldness talked about the books he was reading, and the great job he is doing in his career. I loved every minute of it because this is what I do. I like connecting with winners. I knew he was winning. I knew from the handshake and the way he looked me in my eyes that he had greatness all over him. We continued to go back and forth as you do in these settings for almost 10 minutes and finally I was pulled into another conversation. While engaged in the next conversation, I had this thought pop in and out of my mind, "What is this young man doing in this private members bar?"

Oh, if I might add, his Uncle told me he was thoroughly impressed with my speech and his nephew needed someone like myself to be involved in his continued development. I passed him a card and didn't think anything else of the evening. A few days later I receive a call from Kenneth Smith requesting a meeting with me. I replied with a day and time and we met.

Today, you're holding in your hands the first of many best-selling books from Author, Kenneth Smith Jr. Kenneth is doing amazing things and is definitely on the fast track of success. His hunger to help, his drive to dream, and his humble teachable spirit makes him one of today's top millennial thought leaders in America. He's innovative, multi-talented, with multiple streams of income, Kenneth understands the importance of being in authority and still under authority.

Today, I have the awesome privilege of being his Transformational Coach so with great honor I introduce and part the stage so you can too find out what I have grown to know and respect --- the knowledge and wisdom of Kenneth Smith, Jr.

assistu2win.com

derricklbutts.com

derrickb@assistu2win.com

No matter your age or stage, race or place, whatever you do: GO WIN!

Introduction

Hello, my name is Kenneth Smith, Jr. I want to personally thank you for taking time out to read my first book, and I hope it greatly impacts your life.

Growing up, I did not listen to anyone. I quit on many of my commitments, and the result was that by the time I was 18, I acted as if I was five years old. The crazy part was that growing up, I wanted to do the right thing and to live a good life.

I am writing this book because I messed up, and if it wasn't for me opening my mind and having a few people around me take the time to truly love me and help me develop, even in my worst times, I would have been a complete failure. Although I cannot physically be involved in your life, I desire that me—taking the time out to put this book together for you—will have the same and even greater impact on your life.

As you're reading this book, I want you to remember that no matter where you are in your life, you have hope. If you are not perfect while or after reading this book, no worries because each breath is a new beginning, and no one is perfect to begin with. The main difference between winners and losers is that losers quit. You will never get to where you want to be if you quit. Everyone falls, but champions get back up. Are you a champion? YES! So, let's get back up, and make things happen!

Chapter 1:
Value Advice

Listening to proper authority will always give you the quickest access to maturity, and you will reap the most benefits. An example of proper authority would be a parent, teacher, coach, mentor, etc. Although listening to proper authority can be annoying and boring, it will be one of the best decisions in your life.

Value Advice

Growing up

Growing up, I didn't listen to much my parents said. *Whether* that was because they weren't "cool" enough, not spiritual enough, didn't have enough money, not enough fame, etc. the list could go on and on. Although they labored tremendously to bring me into this world, I had not much honor for them.

See, my parents tried for 10 years to have me until my dad found out he could not have kids due to a rare issue. So, what he did—because he wanted to have me so badly—was have a surgery that was going to put him in the worst pain of his life, according to the doctors, for three days... and even after that, it would still be a risk as to whether I would be conceived.

After he had the surgery, my dad then tried again. A few weeks later, the news came in on the same exact day he found out his mom was going to die, that I was going to be born. I was called the miracle baby, and my parents loved me unconditionally. Yet, even after that, I still did not honor my parents. It wasn't just not listening to them; I didn't listen to anybody.

Nobody was able to tell me anything, and I wanted to learn everything for myself without listening, which was a huge issue.

Not listening didn't go so well.

I suffered horribly because I did not listen growing up. Not listening caused me to act like I was five years old when I was 18 years old. It wasn't that I just didn't listen to my parents; I didn't listen to advice period. Not listening will cause you to be immature because the only way you can mature is by listening. You can either listen to proper authority, listen to the voice of rebellion, or listen to your past experiences.

Listening to proper authority:

Listening to proper authority will always give you the quickest access to maturity and will equip you with the most benefits. An example of proper authority would be a parent, teacher, coach, mentor, etc. Although listening to proper authority can be annoying and boring, it will be one of the best decisions in your life.

The voice of rebellion :

Listening to the voice of rebellion is the worst choice because you listen to a voice you know is wrong, simply for a selfish reward. When you listen to the voice of rebellion, you go directly against what your conscience tells you is the right thing to do. Listening to the voice of rebellion will cause you to hurt other people, unintentionally, while destroying your own life.

Living by experience:

Listening to your mistakes is simply living by experience. This is the slowest way to becoming mature because you listen to nobody. This is probably most common in America in 2018 because you constantly hear people saying things like, "Nobody can tell me what to do," and "I just want to try everything and learn it for myself." You want to go through the experience yourself before you ever decide on what you believe.

The first authority in your life:

Your parents are the first authority to come into your life here on earth, and how you treat them is a representation of your life in general. Authority is important, and you must respect and listen to it. Now unfortunately, some people are not born with honorable parents, but still you must honor them for being your parents. Respecting someone does not mean that you must listen to them. You must respect your parents no matter what, but if they are not living an honorable lifestyle, then you need to find someone who does and listen to them. But that honor part is important because everything you do in life is a seed.

Not honoring your parents will cost you later in life because how you treat your parents is a seed into how you treat authority. Just because an authority in your life is not honorable, you still must honor them anyway. Dishonor for authority is the reason many people's lives are in the condition they are in. Now dishonor to proper authority in your life causes major setbacks and consequences. Dishonoring my parents caused me to almost be a complete failure in life. Throughout this book you will learn about the things I wish I knew before I turned 18, most of which were actually taught to me and I refused to listen, and some of the things that were not taught to me.

It's amazing how we can be right in front of the very thing we want and reject it. I wanted this wisdom and knowledge that was taught to me when I was younger, but I rejected it. Why did I reject it? Because I thought I knew everything. And the things I didn't know, I wanted to learn through experience. I simply let pride block me, all while I thought I was humble. Humility may be painful, but it is one of the best qualities on earth.

Accept correction.

Getting corrected can be one of the most painful things in life, but it is also one of the most rewarding. Never despise correction. Don't get upset with the person correcting you either because it is an act of love for them to correct you. Having the humility to accept correction is a must have to be successful.

It's not like I never heard good advice.

People were really giving me good advice growing up. I remember being in a finance class my senior year of high school with a teacher named Mr. Smith. This gentleman was an intelligent man, a hard worker, and he was passionate about helping people financially. In this finance class, we took a Dave Ramsey course. At that time, I thought finances were not important at all.

I did not pay attention in class whatsoever and barely passed. I was a fool to do that. I thought Dave Ramsey was not spiritual enough to have a say-so on what I should do with my finances, and I wanted to listen to someone who really heard from God.

Now, a few years later, I actually follow Dave Ramsey and his courses. I also practice his teachings and have great respect for that man. If I only would have listened to the advice I was receiving not only from Mr. Smith, not only from Dave Ramsey, not only from my parents, but from all the other people in my life giving me advice on life after high school, my life would be very different today. We've all heard good advice before. One of the most common things you'll hear adults say is, "I wish I knew that when I was younger." In most cases, someone told them, they just didn't listen.

You can't just listen to anybody.

When you listen to someone you tend to become similar to that person in that area of life, so make sure you choose to listen to the right voice. Now don't go looking for a perfect person to listen to because everyone has flaws. But you don't want to be naïve, so make sure you vet things out first. It is important that you do this because history repeats itself. Nations tend to go down the same paths of failure as previous nations. People on the way to success go through a similar process, etc.

So, if you practice the same principles that led to someone else's success, you are almost guaranteed to have the same success. Many people think that success is luck, but it is really your decisions that determine the success you have. *The first decision you need to make in life is to acknowledge that you don't know everything and just listen.*

Then, find someone who has the success you desire and listen to them. You must seek wisdom and knowledge, so that you can grow and be a mature adult without screwing your life up first. You are transformed by the changing of your mind. *Napoleon Hill stated that if you change the way you think, then you will be successful.*

The information you have now has led to the life you currently live. You are going to need new information to get you to the next level. Your success in life is based off decisions and not luck. Therefore, who you choose to listen to and associate with is extremely important.

So, what do you do?

One of the best things about living in the 21st century is the access to information. No matter who you are, because of technology you can get access to tremendous amounts of valuable information. Now, with that comes the access to a lot of bad information on the Internet as well, but it's up to you to choose what you're going to listen to. Of course, it is never too late to change, and that is one of the reasons why I'm writing this book to encourage you that no matter the bad choices you've made, you can have a new start today.

The first decision you must make to have a new start is you have to listen. Mike Murdock says *"**your future depends on who you believe. If you show me who you believe, I will show you your future.**"* That statement is so true because when all I believed was my own voice, I made childish decisions that led to failure. Why do most people not want to listen? It is because listening takes faith and trust, so you must trust that person in order to listen to them. But to have success in life, you must take risks. I also encourage you today to find a proven mentor and follow their advice.

Chapter 2:

Can't Live Without Discipline

The main difference between a kid and an adult is discipline. A kid does whatever he or she wants, while an adult does what needs to get done. As an adult you're going to have to do things that you don't want to do, such as go to work when you don't want to, clean the house when you don't want to, and many more things when you don't feel like doing them.

Can't Live Without Discipline

The main difference between a kid and an adult...

The main difference between a kid and an adult is discipline. A kid does whatever he or she wants, while an adult does what needs to get done. As an adult you're going to have to do things you don't want to do, such as go to work when you don't want to, clean the house when you don't want to, and many more things when you don't feel like doing them.

Discipline effects everything.

How disciplined you are definitely affects all aspects of your life. An undisciplined person will be too lazy to get anything done in life. A key area of your life that discipline affects is your focus. Without discipline you will not be able to focus on anything. If you are unable to focus on anything, then you won't be able to succeed as an adult because you won't be able to finish anything.

The ability to say "NO":

As an adult you will have many distractions, but if you want to live a successful life, then you must have the discipline to be able to finish the things you start. You must be able to say "no" to things as an adult. A mature person has the power to say "no" to distractions that come into their life. An immature person can't help but give into the temptation to any and everything that comes their way. You must always remember that you cannot please everyone. Mature adults love others, and still manage to not allow others' opinions to affect their decisions. You can't say "yes" to everyone who asks you for something, and you can't say "yes" to every opportunity.

Work requires discipline.

You need discipline in order to put in work. Work is vital because if you don't work, then you won't be productive. If you are not productive, then you won't fulfill your purpose in life. If you are not fulfilling your purpose in life, then you will feel void. You won't always feel like picking up the phone to make that sales call or take out the trash, but you must have the discipline to do it even when you don't feel like it. Work is very vital to a person's life, and it is the reason why many people are either happy or sad. If you don't have enough work in your life, you will be sad. I call that "the crippled life".

The crippled life:

Have you ever met someone who is very depressed, always angry at people, hates the world, barely has any physical energy, loves to sleep, never does anything for other people, etc.? I'm pretty sure we all have met one person like that. Well, that lifestyle can be attributed to a lack of self-discipline.

Growing into a baby:

The older I got, I started to become more immature when I stopped listening to my parents. My parents didn't know what to do, so they decided to just support me in whatever decision I made. As hard as it is to say it, they babied me. They made me any meal I wanted, they did my chores for me, and they allowed me to do whatever I wanted. Growing up, I was harder on myself than my parents were on me. I am not blaming them, though, because they simply did not know what to do.

Letting go of discipline led me into depression.

At one point when I was a teenager, I genuinely thought I wouldn't have to be disciplined like I was before. I thought God would take care of me, since I started to really believe in Him, which was a terrible mistake. I became like a four-year-old. I literally could not take care of myself. I let go of discipline, and I had no one to keep me in line, so it led to my world falling apart.

During this time, I fell into depression and started to just barely pass school, and I failed most assignments. I became someone with a total lack of discipline, and the results almost led to me losing my mind. Although doing whatever you want may seem awesome, it is absolutely horrifying the results that occur. Doing whatever you want is tempting, but if you want to live in depression, just become undisciplined.

Handle your own business.

As an adult it is important to be able to handle your own business. Others will not be able to take care of you as an adult. *The whole point of being considered an adult is being able to manage your own life and the responsibilities you have, such as your house, family, and finances.* You are not an adult if you are unable to manage your own life.

Discipline equals money.

If you are undisciplined, you will never grow in finances. Not only will you not grow in finances, but if you do have money, without discipline you won't be able to manage it. When I first moved out on my own, I was undisciplined in the area of finances. I lost track of how much I purchased, I didn't make a budget, and made many other poor financial mistakes. Because of my lack of discipline in the way I handled my finances, I remained financially broke. I also became untrustworthy to others and unreliable with money. I also made false promises and let people down. With discipline, people can trust and rely on you in situations.

Discipline will reward you with respect.

People will respect you for being a disciplined person. On top of respect, you will also get success. It requires discipline to get success.

Discipline brings a happy life.

Discipline will also reward you with happiness. You would think that the people who do what they want to do would be the happiest but, no, it is the people who are the most disciplined who are the happiest. With being disciplined, you simply become a happy person from the inside-out, and you start to be pleased with life as well. Everyone wants to be successful, but the discipline it may take to be successful may hurt physically and be boring temporarily. However, over time, it will leave you with a sustained amount of happiness. People who are disciplined are not just pleased with their external life like cleanliness, work life, and marriage, but they also are happy internally because discipline is a fruit of a healthy heart spiritually.

But don't get burnt-out.

It is easy in life to get burnt-out. Sometimes we can be so excited about work and go too overboard with discipline that we burn out. For example, one time I was doing a fast from any food or drink I liked, so I only ate very healthy foods that taste nasty and did it for too long. While on the fast, I saw productivity and growth, so I liked it and thought that I can do it for the rest of my life, but it was mentally overbearing for me. Another example is me trying to work out for two or three hours every day for years because I thought I didn't need rest. I eventually got burnt-out from the harsh workouts and stopped working out for a while. I wanted to always do what I didn't want to do, simply so I will never have the feeling of not wanting to do something, but that's not even true discipline.

True discipline:

Discipline is doing simply what you don't want to do, to achieve something that you need or want. True discipline will give you a balanced life. You'll be able to balance recreational time, family time, work time, cleaning time, and more, so that you will be able to get all the things you need done and be happy. Discipline is when you are eating a delicious dessert and have the power to stop at a certain point, instead of over-eating.

Discipline affects relationships.

Discipline will help you build meaningful and sustained relationships. When I was younger, I didn't have the discipline to stop speaking when I needed to stop, nor did I have the power to not say the things I shouldn't say. The result was that I spoke whatever came to mind and, because of that, not many people wanted to be around me. Not everybody wants to hear every thought that comes to your mind. It also takes discipline to continue being someone's friend after years of pain.

Establish good habits.

Discipline will help you form one of the most important things in your life, which are good habits. Having good habits equals having a good life. Good habits will produce the life you've always wanted. Your life is simply the sum total of your habits. To form those good habits, you need to have discipline. For example, when I was younger, I used to have a habit of working out consistently. It was pretty much impossible for me to not work out daily, and I'm so thankful because it has kept me in a healthy body. People want to change their life, but they need to know that it's just the simple little habits that will give them the life they want. But in order to create those good habits, you need discipline.

Discipline is your life.

It is important to apply discipline in all areas of your life. You need to make that the core value of your life, for it is your life. Without discipline, you won't be able to achieve anything in life.

What to do now?

If you truly know the importance of discipline, you will make sure you always have the following attribute, which will result in a successful life. If you are looking for a change in your life, begin to implement discipline as much as you can, even if it's something little. For example, being consistent with brushing my teeth, morning and night, helped instill discipline in me. Although I didn't have much discipline, simply brushing my teeth consistently was a start for me, and eventually I was able to be disciplined over my whole life. If you are much further in life than I was, you can implement working out on a consistent basis. Working out is a phenomenal way to increase discipline, and being consistent with it is the icing on the cake. **Simply implement one habit that you can stay consistent with for over 90 days. Do this to help build discipline.**

Chapter 3:

Live with Awareness

Kids do whatever they want, whenever they want, not even considering the consequences. As an adult, you must be aware of your surroundings because if you don't, your life will fall apart.

Live with awareness

You must have a sense of awareness.

Kids do whatever they want, whenever they want, not even considering the consequences. As an adult, you must be aware of your surroundings because if you don't, your life will fall apart.

Pay attention to the details.

In 2018 America, it seems as if paying attention to details is a bad thing. People call others "OCD" and make fun of them if they are obsessed with the details. But, paying close attention to details is crucial to your survival. As an adult, you will have responsibilities that must be taken care of, or else your life will fall apart. Every day people die because of simple carelessness and living unaware. Why do you think a Rolls Royce costs more than a Toyota? The details. Details matter, and attention to details provides value.

Key things to be aware of always:

Bills

You will have bills that must be paid on time. To pay your bills effectively, you need to be aware. You need to be aware that those bills do exists, what day they are due, how much is due, and what is due. This is crucial to your life because it not only applies to your personal life, but it also applies to those around you. If you live unaware, then you will let others down constantly, making false promises, not paying your bills, living unclean, and putting a burden on those around you to take care of you. You will have kids who rely on you to keep the lights on and pay the bills. If you are unaware of when a bill is due, and how much is due, then you may not be able to pay the bill on time, which could result in putting your life and your family's lives on the line. See, that's what living unaware does; it creates unexpected disasters.

Relationships

Always pay close attention to your relationships. You want to consistently nurture every meaningful relationship in your life. A lack of meaningful relationships is the reason many people are depressed, homeless, or bitter. You want to nurture your friendships, marriage, business connections, and children.

Health

Pay close attention to your health because living unhealthy is the number one reason people are dying in America. Unhealthy living is simply suicide on a payment plan.

Appointments

Always keep track of the appointments you have on your schedule because by missing them you waste not only your time, but other people's time as well. You also waste money when you miss appointments.

Time

Keep track of your time because you can never get it back. Time is precious, so use your time wisely.

Money

Keep careful watch of your finances. Always know your income, how much you are spending, what you are spending your money on, what is in your bank account currently, and where your money is at any given time.

Just because you can, doesn't mean you should.

Just because you're physically capable of doing something, does not mean that it's good to do it. For example, you should not eat a gallon of ice cream at two in the morning, right before you go to bed, when you must wake up for work at 6:00am. There are consequences when eating ice cream that late. If you know you must work in the morning, don't stay out until 5:00 a.m. if you have go to work at eight. Although the moment may be fun, you do more damage than good to your life by making such an unwise decision, simply because you were living unaware.

You must protect yourself.

You are your own security guard over your life. No one is going to care for your things as much as you do. No one else is going to protect you the way you want. No one will love you exactly the way you want either. No one can give you anything and everything you want, so you must love and nurture yourself.

You must be a guard over your life. You don't want to lose the things you have, so you must always keep a sense of awareness. Like a security guard, you must always be alert and ready for action. And I'm not just talking about burglars breaking into your home, I'm talking about every enemy that comes against an important area of your life. For example, you must watch for and cut-off laziness, unhealthy relationships, negative words, carelessness, poverty, and other negative things that will come against you and your family. You must be aggressive about getting rid of your weaknesses and anything negative that would come against you.

You can help others.

When you are always on alert and live a responsible life, you then are in a position where you can begin to help others, as well as yourself. If someone gets into trouble, then you could possibly help them get out. But, if you are unaware, even if you were to recognize that person's needs, you will possibly not be able to help them because your own life is out of order. However, most likely, you will not even be able to recognize that they need help because you are unaware.

Others are depending on you.

Others will be depending on you as an adult. You will have a family that loves and cares about you, and because of that you can't let them down. Other people will also believe in and want to see the best for you, so don't let them down either. Here's how. You live life aware of your surroundings and simply stay responsible. Your business connections will also be counting on you to come through on your promises.

Too much sleep is dangerous.

Getting too much sleep can lead to an unaware life. Responsible people don't oversleep. It's okay to have a night where you sleep for a very long time occasionally, but too much sleep on a consistent basis will lead to poverty. I'm not saying sleep is bad because everyone needs it, and it is vital to your productivity, but what I am saying is that oversleeping and getting too much sleep can be destructive. **Most people oversleep simply because they want to escape their life's problems.** They don't want to be aware of the problems that are currently in their life, but that is very immature. This was me for a period of time, and I wished I could be somewhere else in a dream away from my reality. Some people say they just like to sleep, but I have never met anyone who was truly mature or excited about life who constantly overslept.

Too much partying is dangerous.

On top of not oversleeping, you must make sure you don't party too much. In other words, party smart. Partying is good. It is good to let go and have fun, but you need to have a good balance to work hard and play hard. It's good for your emotions and your body to relax and have fun, but it is not good to go overboard with it. For example, drinking too much can be destructive. I have a friend who drank too much at a party, and to this day—because of that night—he is still paralyzed in a wheelchair. If he would've been responsible enough to know when to stop, he would still be a healthy young man today.

Be prepared for any and everything.

You need to always be prepared for the good and the worse. You need to be prepared for the best thing to ever happen in your life because it can literally happen today, tomorrow, or whenever. People wish for things, but their lives are not ready to contain whatever it is if it was to come.

You also need to prepare for the worst in life. Most people in America do not want to hear that, but it is true. You need to be prepared for the worst. It is essential to your survival. As an adult, you can't just think about making it; you must think about the possibilities that would be good or bad.

Get organized.

Organization is important as an adult. You need to know where things go and where things are. If you're not organized, you won't be aware. If you're organized, then you will be aware. And, things will be plain and simple. With being organized, you will be very tempted to go back into a state of fantasy— wanting to escape life's problems—because you will be very aware of everything in your life. You will notice that people who are unorganized and equally messy with their work, words or time, usually have lives that are both unorganized and messy, personally as well.

Don't try to escape life.

Adults don't run from problems; they solve them. You just can't slip back into trying to escape from your life. If you do try to escape, your life will collapse and escape from you. Therefore, it will be miserable.

I did this once when I was 19-years-old. I started to overeat simply to escape life. Although overeating may not seem bad, doing it to escape your current situation is the same as doing drugs, smoking, drinking, or having too much sex. Everything in my life got worse when I did that, but thank God I never gave up and had support from the people who were around me. I am now stronger than ever, and I now know the importance of having a healthy balance of work, rest, and play.

Through it all, you must fight for your awareness because many things will try to come against it. Nations have lost wars; people have lost homes; and so many more negative outcomes have happened simply because an individual was unaware.

What to do?

The first thing you want to do is spend a week organizing your life. Set the order. Remember, you are your own CEO, so you must take charge and put things in their place. Organize your room, office, relationships, finances, time, appointments, bills, etc. When you come home at night, instead of just placing everything that is in your pocket on the counter, have a designated place in your room where those items go. Also, get a parent, mentor, or friend to help keep you accountable.

Since your awareness is not fully developed, you need someone who is aware and successfully managing their own life to help keep you on track. That person does not have to be intricately involved in every detail of your life; however, you do need someone to check up on you and to see how you are doing in specific areas, also giving correction where it is needed. You then want to slowly cut back on every distraction, such as overeating, oversleeping, too much TV, etc. If you do these three things, it will be hard for you to become unaware of your life again.

Chapter 4:

The Basic Know-How's

Mommy and daddy are not going to be there to take care of you and to do things for you all the time, so you need to learn how to take care of yourself. As an adult you must know certain things; there are no exceptions unless you have a disability.

The Basic Know-How's

A grown baby

When I was 18-years-old, I was going on five. I had the same amount of knowledge on how to do practical things as some five-year olds. I didn't know how to do basic things that you need to know how to do in life such as mop, sweep, and eat properly. The result of this was a lot of issues for myself and those around me. I needed to establish the simple daily habits that you need to get through life at 18-years-old simply because I refused to listen to my parents when I was growing up. It's one thing to just know how to do something, but it's another thing to actually do it, and sadly enough I didn't have either.

Waiting till you get older to learn?

You were meant to become a successful adult who can manage your own life. As soon as a baby is born, the parents immediately begin to help it mature, eventually into an adult. To say that you will wait to learn to do something that is vital to your life, is not good. Procrastination cannot be in your life as an adult. So, you might as well learn what you need to know now, so you won't have to worry about the pain later. Mommy and Daddy are not going to be there to take care of and to do things for you all the time, so you need to learn how to take care of yourself. As an adult, you must know certain things. There are no exceptions, unless *maybe* you have a disability. I'm going to name some things you must know how to do as an adult and should expect to learn if you don't already know.

Things you need to know:

Take care of your body and groom yourself.

You need to know how to take care of your body. You need to know how to take showers, brush your teeth properly, floss, wash your face, wash and comb/brush your hair, shave, and clip your nails. You especially need to know things that are gender-specific and pertain to your own private body parts.

How to clean:

You need to know how to clean. Here are the basic things for when it comes to cleaning. They are:

- Know how to sweep and mop the floor;
- Know how to scrub off a spot on the counter;
- Know how to clean dishes;
- Know how to stack dishes;
- Know how to file;
- Know how to organize a room;
- Know how to vacuum;
- Know how to clean your furniture and other items in your home;
- Know how to wash, dry and put away your clothes properly;
- Know how to wash your car; and,
- Know how to clean the inside of your car.

Make sure you know what you need to clean and how to clean it well today.

Keep up with technology.

Some of the things you know, you may only need for one generation; however, it doesn't matter because if it is vital to your survival, then you still need to learn it, even if you only needed to know it for one year. Many people don't want to learn things, such as how to use a computer, simply because they don't want to keep up with technology. That is not a wise decision.

You need to learn how to use a computer because a computer is involved in almost every aspect of business, marketing, and relationships. The computer is where people connect. It is where people buy things and where people talk. You also need to know how to use a computer on most jobs, and there are many other reasons to learn to use one. The same goes with all technology that are must-haves, such as the cell phone.

Here are other technologies you need to know how to use. You must know how to use a computer, a cell phone, a printer, and a washer/dryer.

Learn how to drive.
You need to learn how to drive a car. The main way people get around these days is in a car, so you need to learn. Not only should you know how to drive a car, but you need to know how to take care of your car as well. You must know how to change a spare tire, check your oil, clean the inside and outside of the car, and check

the engine, plus read check engine lights.

How to cook:

Everyone should know how to cook, to some degree. You don't have to become a master chef, but at least have one to three dishes that you can cook well.

How to communicate:

You need to know how to communicate effectively, which means knowing how to read, write, and speak properly. But, communication is much more than just being verbal. The non-verbal side of communication is even more important.

These are the things you need to learn when it comes to communication. You need to learn:

- Proper manners for the culture you are in;
- How to dine at a table elegantly;
- How to treat strangers;
- How to take feedback;
- How to say "no" respectfully
- How to correct someone respectfully;
- How to make small talk;
- How to apologize;

- How to speak to your spouse;
- How to speak in front of authority;
- How to treat the opposite gender;
- **How to speak to a group/crowd;**
- How to speak to those under your authority;
- How to read and write; and,
- How to type at least 30 words per minute.

Your money-making skill:

You need to learn your money-making skill as soon as possible. What skill can you master that people will pay you for? This is something you must know because, without money, you won't be able to buy food, which will allow you to live. You need to learn a skill that will makes you money.

How to handle finances

Growing up, I was very irresponsible. I almost always dropped or lost something. That carried over into my finances when I got older. I constantly lost money and didn't know where my money went. I didn't know how to handle cash. Until I was 20, I didn't really know what a credit card was. When it comes to finances, you need to know the difference between a debit card and a credit card, how to handle cash, what taxes are, what it means to invest, the difference between an income and an expense, the difference between a withdrawal and a deposit, and different investment options (i.e. stocks, bonds, forex, mutual funds, etc.).

Your life's purpose:

The most important thing to know in life is your purpose. Not everyone has the same purpose in life. Matter a fact, no one does. Not everyone considers being a millionaire a successful life. Some people just want to have a great marriage and a healthy family, and once they achieve that—even though they are not millionaires—they will feel complete.

Once you find out what your life purpose is, you will then know what you consider to be a successful life for yourself. You will also be able to create and put goals into place and have a vision in front of you to run with. It is so important that you know what your purpose in life is because if you don't, then you will go from one thing to another, trying to reach for something you will never get because you don't know what you're looking for. When you know your life's purpose, you will begin to feel meaningful and purposeful, not dead.

What to do?

I have provided you with many things you need to know in order to live a successful life. Now that we have Google, libraries and elders, I'm not going to list the definitions and details of everything; that is for you to research. Do your research on these things, and if you know and understand all the things I have listed, then you will be able to live as a responsible adult.

Chapter 5

Money is Important

You need money to survive. If you don't have money, then you can't buy food, shelter, or clothes. It takes money to have these essential things that you need to survive in life. You should want money so that you will be able to survive and thrive, and not only for you, but also for your family, so that you can provide.

Money is Important

I didn't want money.

I grew up thinking money was not important. I was so unaware of money growing up that I actually didn't even want any until I was 19-years-old. Growing up, my parents gave me pretty much anything I wanted, so I wasn't even aware of money or the work it took to get it because of the easy access I had to it. On the positive side, I did have great compassion for others who were less fortunate, financially. My parents would always offer to buy me nice things, but I never wanted it. When I was younger, I would always say I couldn't wait to grow up and just give away all my money to the poor because of the great compassion I had for others.

Then everything changed.

When I turned 19, I moved out of my parents' house. I truly believe I was making the right decision by moving out because of the situation I was in. But, I recommend staying with your parents until you are financially well-off. When I moved into my new apartment, I was only working as a salesman at Macy's making $7.55 an hour. At the end of the month rent came around, and I wasn't sure if I had enough. I was one month into living on my own and already feeling the pains of financial struggle. It was confusing to me because I felt like I was doing the right thing by living there, and that I was being a good person. Thankfully, I had just enough money to pay the rent for that month.

As each month went by, money got tighter and tighter. I didn't know how I was going to pay my bills, and I was short on rent. On top of not being able to pay bills, I didn't have the money to buy food. It made no sense to me because I prayed more than I ever had in my life. I was doing my best to become a better man.

I noticed that although I was being nice and not doing bad things, being a good person didn't affect my financial situation. At the same time, I knew that there was something wrong with being broke. I was very confused, because I thought money would just be given to me, and that I would always have enough and more. I was oblivious to money growing up, and it carried over when I moved out.

That's when I began to realize the importance of being knowledgeable in the area of finances because poverty is the reason why people steal, stress, starve, and even sometimes kill. I also realized money doesn't just fall off trees, and that it is my decisions/work ethic that determine my income.

You need money to live.

You need money in order to survive. If you don't have money, then you can't buy food, shelter, or clothes. It takes money to have the essential things that you need to survive in life. You should want money, so that you will be able to survive and thrive, and not only for you, but also for your family, so that you can provide.

It's not evil to want money.

It's actually a contradiction to say it's evil to want money. If you care the slightest bit about anyone, including yourself, then you should want money because, if someone doesn't have money they cannot eat, nor will they have a home.

Coming to the awareness of money.

It takes some people extreme situations for them to come to the awareness of money. For example, a person is stranded outside in the winter in -5°F weather with no clothes. In due time, that person can freeze to death just like many people have in history unless he buys warm clothes and seeks shelter. That person may have never seen the value of having money until he realized that if he had the money to buy some clothes and pay for a home, then he could save his life.

It's natural to want money.

It's natural and good for us to want money. How do I know? Because it is natural for someone to hate poverty and want to give to the poor. If you have those feelings and thoughts of compassion and love for the poor, and a passion for wanting to end poverty, then you should really want money because it's going to take money to end poverty.

With more money you can help more people. When my friends and I went to help the homeless, what we provided them with had cost us money. I learned a lot from going out on the streets with them to help the homeless and spend time with them. We used to go pretty much every week. I've seen people in 25° freezing weather with no shelter. And a lot of these people are not crazy; they were people just like me and you who made a few mistakes, and for some of them it was just one costly mistake too much. One of those mistakes for most was not seeing money as important. The reason they are homeless is because they do not have enough money to pay for shelter. If you and I make more money, then we can provide more homes for these people.

You get to help yourself.

One of the most painful things I've ever experienced in life was having to go to Taco Bell because I could not afford Panera bread or some food of quality. It made me so sad because since I didn't have enough money, I could not feed my body properly enough. Poverty makes you not care or value yourself. That's why you see people who are poor live and act the way they do, and some are seen as crazy. But it's only because the lack of money has caused such an overall low self-esteem that they lose themselves.

When you cannot afford to buy things like soap, food and clothes, it can negatively affect you mentally, if you let it. People, when they become poor, sometimes stop cleaning, stop taking care of themselves, become money-hungry, lose relationships, or even become addicted to substances—like drugs or alcohol—all because of the hopeless feeling they have, since they did not have enough money or resources to **take care** of themselves properly.

Money gives you credibility.

If you don't care about humanity, there is still a reason you should want money because it gives you credibility. You can be correct in whatever you are speaking about but, if you're poor, it's more likely that people won't listen to you. If you're rich, you're much more likely to have people to listen when you speak. Influence and credibility are important because you have something inside you that is important and must be given to the world. In order for you to persuade people, you need credibility, which also means you will need access to money and what it offers.

You can give back.

With money you can give back to your parents, elders, hometown, or whoever has poured into you. Whether they were leaders, simply older family members, or friends who poured into you in some way, you can bless them back with money, or by buying them something. You can never go wrong with having a lot of money and doing good things, but you can go wrong with being broke. Not having money is a real-life curse.

Money makes you happy

Although money can't give you ever-lasting joy, having plenty of it can make you happy. You can't tell me that going to Six Flags, or doing something you, your friends, and your family loves and thinks is fun, does not make you happy! Although people will acknowledge that going to a concert is fun, they don't acknowledge that it was money that was able to buy them the tickets.

Money does really make you happy. Whenever I had very little money, just a few dollars left in my account, I was up most of the time stressed and filled with low self-esteem. But when I had a lot of money, I felt a lot of confidence and was happy because it gave me options. Options   are   good!

Money attracts friends.

No one wants to hang around someone who is broke unless they are broke, too. Poverty repels friends, but money attracts them. Ever had a friend who constantly begged for money? I'm sure you two are not close friends anymore because, as an individual, it is our responsibility to take care of our own business. You wouldn't want your friends to be a burden on you right!? Then don't become a burden on them.

Become a person who attracts money.

I suggest that everyone should invest in themselves. The way I've gotten more money is that I invested in my own personal development because as you grow, you will attract more business towards you. One thing I believed growing up is that I needed to become someone who can attract money because times will change. Eventually my location will change, and things in the economy will not be the same way they are today. But there are principles to wealth.

There are principals a person can follow that, if you follow them too, can cause you to be rich in any society at any time. Businesses around the world go bankrupt every day. See, you can't trust one company to always provide you a job because as we have seen over the past hundred years, business has changed, companies have gone bankrupt, natural disasters occur, and people have lost jobs for reasons that are not their fault. So, you must become someone who can go out and attract money. **You must know your money-making skill well and sharpen your knowledge day by day.**

It's not wrong to want a profit.

I used to think if I was to do something and get something in return, then I have evil motives. That's not true. You need to reap what you sow; it is natural law. I now think it's wrong to put so much effort into something and not want something back. The only time it's not wrong to want something in return is when you're giving a gift. Mature people know they need to bring home a profit. If you don't have money, then you can't pay your bills. And to bring home a profit, you must want to get something in return.

Be practical.

Money is something you can't be in "la la land" about. Money is not love. If you don't have it written, then you're not serious. If you can't show statistically on paper how you will reach your goal, then you will more than likely not reach your goal. Become a detail-oriented person and take the necessary steps to become financially established and financially independent.

Time is precious, so don't waste it.

Successful people know how to use their time better and more efficient. Time is very important, so you must use it wisely. I remember when I did not use my time wisely. I used to just live sloppily, but that's why I was unsuccessful.

What to Do?

If you are currently in financial trouble, or in a place where you are unaware of money, then begin to invest into your own personal development. Begin reading books on finances that will help you grow in that area. Think practical. Can you truly afford the lifestyle you're living? What about downsizing for a few years, so you can save and invest more money? Put everything on paper, and budget yourself to financial freedom within a certain amount of time. With finances, if you don't have it written, then your dreams will always simply be dreams that do not become reality.

Chapter 6

Value Relationships

Everything you ever wanted is in a relationship. All the love you want in life is through a relationship. All the money you want is through a relationship. Meaningful and special moments are created through

Value Relationships

Relationships are extremely valuable.

Relationships are essential to your life. Just think; everything you ever wanted is in a relationship. All the love you want in life is through a relationship. All the money you want is through a relationship. Meaningful and special moments are created through relationships. At the end of your life, you will look back on the times you enjoyed with someone. When you begin to realize the value of relationships, you start to live differently. You start to take little things more seriously because you know how much they affect your relationships.

My communication flaws as a kid.

When I was a kid, I did not invest in myself when it came to my relational skills. I actually went backwards because I began to think it was cool to be ghetto for much of my young life. I had poor communication skills, and I did not walk with confidence... constantly walking with a slouch and my head hanging down. If you saw me, I was always twitching and looked like something was wrong with me. I always thought about myself and not about the other person. I always spoke when I wanted to, not considering what the other person had to say, and I didn't listen when other people spoke—whether that be an authority or a friend, it did not matter. When other people told me they didn't like when I did something, I thought they needed to get themselves together and truly love me for who I am. I repelled people from me instead of attracting them.

Money made me realize.

I first discovered that I needed to invest in my relational skills when I first became aware of money. When you are short on rent, you become aware of how important money is. And when you become aware of how important money is, you begin to take the necessary steps in order to get the money you need. Me not wanting a quick fix, I knew I needed to invest in myself to be able to get the money I need, not just for now but for my lifetime. When I realized that all money was coming through someone else, I also realized that I needed to invest in my communication and relationship skills. If I can build trust with someone and communicate properly with them to sell myself, then the person might give me their money for a service I would provide. But, if I lack in communication skills, that person might also not buy my product or service— no matter what my product or service is—because they simply do not trust me or like me. I now believe communication should be studied as much as anything else in school, and that it is a shame that it is not taken seriously in school either.

Various reasons to learn communication:

You need to learn how to communicate properly for various reasons that are essential to your life. Even if you simply want to get married, you need to learn how to communicate. If you don't know how, then you won't be able to attract anyone to you.

If you plan on staying married, then you definitely need to learn good communication skills. If you communicate properly, even as a kid, you will be able to get more favor with your teachers in school. If you want to be a good athlete, you need to learn how to communicate with your coach. If you want to be a good pastor, you need to learn how to communicate with your congregation and each individual member.

Communication is not just verbal.

The way you carry yourself even deals with communication. In 1971, Professor Albert Mehrabian concluded that communication is only seven percent verbal and 93 percent non-verbal. The non-verbal was made up of body language (55 percent) and tone of voice (38 percent). **Which tells us that learning non-verbal communication is important as well.**

The value of intimacy:

Just take a look at people who live life without relationships. People who have been alone their whole life, locked away somewhere, are very emotionally unhealthy. There is also a void that you get when you don't have meaningful relationships in your life. I went a few weeks one time shutting out the people who were close to me, and I felt purposeless. You can make a lot of money, be famous, and have all the material things in this world, but without intimacy in your life, you will feel empty and a void. Intimacy is needed in everyone's life. Intimacy is not sex, although sex can be an expression of intimacy. Intimacy is when you can stand in front of someone with nothing to hide and yet still love each other.

The first intimate relationship in life:

Parents must know that their child's first relationship in life is with them. So, how you interact with your child is crucial because our lives are pretty much the result of what we have seen other people do. Doesn't mean you have to do what they do, but you form your opinions, values and beliefs simply off other people's actions, values, and beliefs. So, children must have good interaction with their parents, and they must honor their parents as well. How you raise and show love to your child, most of the time, determines the lifestyle that kid will live.

Honor is gold.

If you learn to honor your parents, you will already be ahead of most people in life because many people don't know how to honor anymore. Honor is something that is missing in today's society. Children need to know that they need to cherish their parents because they will remember the moments with them for the rest of their lives. Also, if it wasn't for their parents, they would not be on earth today. It was a sacrifice—to some degree—for the parents to keep the child through labor and raising them.

Respect those who have supported you. That could be a parent, grandparent, business leader, church leader, or whoever has invested time in you. You need to respect them and pour back into them. There is a broken law that occurs when you do not show gratefulness and honor to those who have invested in you.

Family is treasure.

Family is very important in a child's life because family helps build your love muscle. Knowing you must have someone around you and still love them is very tough. When you can't make somebody leave, you have to either love them or hate them. So, that exercises the love muscle. I believe that broken families are the reason a lot of people walk around with cold hearts and void of love. If you had a family at any point in your life, you always remember the moments you've had with them. Establishing good connections with your family members is very important because they will always be there. You can always count on family, to a degree.

Have Friends:

Building solid friendships is very important to your life because those friendships will help you create fun moments. Friends will really be there for you, take away loneliness, make you feel valuable, and help you enjoy life more as a whole. There is a reason why a singer said, ***"Once I was seven years old, my mama told me, 'go out and make some friends, or you'll be lonely.'"*** Healthy friendships take away the feelings of loneliness.

Friends will be there to support you, encourage you, correct you, and love you. I'm thankful that I was not shy when I was young because I know I can keep in touch with a lot of my old friends. It is good to know that because since they're still in my life to a degree, I always have someone I can go to when I want to hangout or need help, a laugh, or a hug. **Just don't be quick to cut people off, which is a mistake I have made in my life a few times. Learn how to separate peacefully.**

The joy of blessing someone else:

Seeing someone happy from something you've done for them is one of the most blissful things in life.

Long-lasting relationships:

Long-lasting relationships are one of the biggest joys of life. Building it may be hard during the process, but enduring it produces a meaningful and happy life.

You need relationships.

So, not only should you want relationships, but you also need relationships for the betterment of yourself, society, and the other person. You need it for monetary value, spiritual value, and physical value. Relationships are probably the most valuable thing on earth; never take them for granted.

What to do?

I recommend getting counsel from a professional counselor because you will have a safe outlet to pour out your feelings and get wise counsel on how to maintain healthy relationships. Reading self-help books and listening to audio that is dedicated to helping you improve your relationships will also help. Toastmasters International is also something great that you can join to improve your verbal and non-verbal speaking abilities.

Chapter 7:

Love Yourself

It's okay to like who you are, to do things that you like, and to be a person that you like. If you don't like you, then who will? I always think to myself whenever I'm scared of what people will think about me, 'What would the older me appreciate?' That thought helps me live a bold and free life.

Love Yourself

Not selfish to love yourself.

Growing up, I did not love myself because I thought it was selfish, and I was wrong. It is important as an adult that you love yourself because in loving yourself, you take care of yourself. You're only going to take care of things that you love and cherish. **You will not accomplish much in life if you do not love yourself.**

Take care of your body.

It's important that you groom yourself. You need to make sure you not only do the things you need (i.e. brush your teeth, take showers, wash your face, etc.), but you also need to make sure you look nice to you. You need to take care of yourself in a way that makes you really like how you look and makes you happy without breaking the law. You need to do the same for the way you dress, walk, and talk. And, everything you do must be pleasing to you.

You need to really like who you are

It's okay to like who you are, to do things you like, and to be a person you like. If you don't like you, then who will? I always think to myself whenever I'm scared of what people will think about me, *what would the older me appreciate?* That thought helps me live a bold and free life.

Keep everything clean.

Keep the space around you clean; it affects your happiness. If you look around, you might notice that when you don't like your life, things around you are messy. When you are clean and organized, you are much happier with your life and have much more control.

Don't forget to exercise.

It is important that you exercise. Nobody wants to be out of shape, but most Americans are. The reason most people are out of shape is because they would rather have the pleasure of food and laziness, than the benefit of working out. If people can have a good body and be in shape while still having the food and being lazy, they will take it. It is also important to exercise for your mental stability because you exercise discipline. When

I was in sports, I generally was happy. It was not until I quit sports and became idle for a while that I stopped exercising and fell into depression.

Be a positive person.

It is important that you think and speak positively. Now when I say be positive, I don't mean be in La La Land. But what I do mean is this: two people can go outside, and one person says, "Wow, it is such a beautiful day outside." The other person in the same exact situation says, "Wow, I hate life; I hate this world; and I want to die." It's the person's perception that is key. Both people have issues; both have problems; but one chooses to see the good and to be thankful. Two girls who are the same weight look in the same mirror. One says, "I'm beautiful;" the other says, "I'm so fat."

Be thankful.

It is important that we are thankful in our lives for everything we do. Thankfulness is the key to happiness. Learn to want more, but be thankful for what you have. If you are not thankful, you will never be happy.

Smile more.

It is good to smile no matter what gender you are. Smiling naturally makes you happier. I'm not saying to go around smiling all the time, but I am saying it is good for you to smile, and I encourage it. Smiling will help you stay positive even through hard times. It also releases positive vibes to the people around you.

Have healthy relationships.

The people you have around you are a reflection of how much you love yourself and of your life in general. Your relationships are important, so choose wisely who you select to connect with. Don't have people around you who are always speaking negatively about you. There's a difference between correction and being negative all the time. If someone is constantly bringing you down, then you may need to reconsider being their friend, or just distance yourself from them. Be around people who are going to make you smile and make your world better.

Dress nice.

Your clothes are also very important. The clothes you wear make a huge difference in your confidence and in the way you see yourself. If you have on a $20,000 Rolex, you will feel a certain way. If you have a Rolls Royce with an expensive pair of shoes on, you're going to feel differently than if you drove a 1998 Mitsubishi with shoes from Payless. It's not just wearing expensive things; it's looking nicer in your own opinion. I say, "Dress to impress yourself." Don't underestimate, though, the power of dressing to impress other people. How you dress is the first thing people see, so you will attract more quality people by looking nice. Just make sure you like how you are dressed first.

When you appreciate yourself and you like how you look, it makes an extreme impact on your life. Not just your clothes, but things around you. I suggest buying things of quality and not just looking at the price. You begin to see yourself as royalty because at the end of the day that's who you are. You have royalty inside of you. If you are a man, you are king. If you are a woman, you are queen. That's who you are on the inside. When we have nice things, the outside is just a manifestation in the natural of who we are on the inside. So, walk in your royalty, and see yourself as royalty because that's who you are. When a person is fulfilled with things of small value around them, it will be hard for them to truly believe that they are valuable.

Be careful what you share.

You need to watch what you share with other people. People who love themselves do not just share any and everything with everyone. You should not be sharing things that will expose or embarrass you, or anyone else. You also shouldn't share certain blessings that you have with just anyone because it can cause that person's heart to become envious of you. You should not only watch what you share, but also watch who you share it with. Someone who just spits out whatever thought comes to mind simply just doesn't value themselves, or lacks wisdom. You don't share your greatest secrets with just anybody. You also don't devote yourself to just anyone; you're more valuable than that.

Get proper sleep and relaxation.

You need to make sure you're getting proper sleep. Sleep is vital to your happiness and success for the next day. You can't be tired and sleepy while making big decisions. Most people who are sleepless are generally unorganized and not living up to their potential. You need to set aside time not just to sleep, but also to relax. It's also important that your body, mind, soul, and spirit gets time to just relax. You need time to enjoy yourself. Go watch something entertaining—whether that be a movie or a sports game—but whatever it is, make sure that it's very entertaining to you and that you enjoy it. Also do relaxing things like take a nice bubble bath, get a pedicure, or get a massage.

Have fun.

Do not only relax in your downtime, but make sure you have fun in life, too. Go do something fun that you love. Play games with your friends, or go dancing. Simply find something fun you like to do, and be very happy while doing it. Enjoy it to its fullest.

If you are not having any fun in your life, your heart will eventually become bitter because the part of you that wants to have fun has been locked up. Having fun on your downtime is a part of nurturing your body, mind, and soul. I highly suggest getting a hobby that you do weekly. For me, I like to go Salsa/Bachata dancing at least once a week, and I also like to play basketball. A hobby is not only for you to enjoy, but also to keep your mind active, so that you're constantly trying to get better at something you enjoy. A healthy hobby keeps you active, goal-oriented, more stress-free and engaged with people, and in tune with life.

What to do?

Begin to reprogram your mind with healthy thoughts about yourself. Write out a decree about yourself with quotes such as:

- "I am amazing;"
- "I am handsome;" and,
- "I am a winner."

Read it every day. Change what you listen to and read, then make sure it is all uplifting and positive. Also surround yourself with people who are going to speak positively into your life. It is okay to have voices that correct you, but remember that there is a difference between correction and simply being negative. Get a hobby that you enjoy, and do it at least once a week.

Chapter 8:

Integrity

Having good morals and values is a key attribute to having integrity. Although having morals is not something popular these days, you need to have them because it will cause you to live a healthy life. Some examples of good morals and values would be honesty, having courage, making sacrifices, being right and fair, being loyal, having self-respect, respect for others, being forgiving, respecting authority, having patience, making peace, and keeping

Integrity

Integrity is a must.

It is important to have integrity as an adult, and all throughout your life, because if you don't have integrity, then your entire life will eventually fall apart. The reason your life will fall apart is that without integrity, any success you gain will not be authentic. When you don't have integrity, you will spend your whole life simply trying to run from the lies that you have told in the past. A lack of integrity is one of the main reasons why many people's lives are in disarray.

Have good morals and values.

Having good morals and values is one key attribute to having integrity. Although having morals is not seen as popular these days, you need to have them because it will cause you to live a healthy life. ***Some examples of good morals and values are honesty, having courage, making sacrifices, being right and fair, being loyal, having self-respect, having respect for others, being forgiving,*** *respecting authority, having patience, making peace, and keeping promises.*

Those are some examples of having good morals and values. People who live without morals do damage to the people around them while damaging their own life in the process. Living without morals will also get you in trouble with the law. Although you may go a few times without being caught, if you continue living without regard to the law, then you will eventually get caught. As an adult, you must have these attributes to live a meaningful life. You must have these attributes when no one is looking because that is the main point of integrity, which is to do something right even when no one else is looking.

Confession

A part of having integrity is confessing when you know that you did something wrong. When you know that you have messed up and hurt someone, go to that person and tell them you were wrong and that you are sorry. If the person chooses to forgive you, then great. However, if they don't, just move on because they aren't worth being in your life.

When you know that you have done something really wrong on your job, when no one is looking, instead of trying to hide the fact that you did whatever it was, go to your boss and apologize. You will find that bosses love when their employees are completely honest, instead of trying to hide things from them.

Another result of not having integrity is blaming others. Blaming others for the mistakes you have made is weak and is a loser attitude. A person who has integrity acknowledges when they are wrong and takes the blame they deserve, understanding that taking the pain from the blame will cause them to never make that bad decision again. No one is perfect, so you will have to confess a fault at one time or another. Confession is a great attribute to have and will cause other people to trust and like you.

Always welcome correction.

Integrity will allow you to accept correction at the very core of your being because you're not hiding anything. And when you get corrected at the core of who you are, there is then a pureness that flows out of you which will enable you to perform at your best. You will also feel like yourself and be very productive when walking in integrity.

Getting promoted:

Everyone wants to get a promotion at what they do in life, but many people who desire to get promoted try and do so by lying, cheating, murdering, and other ways that do not have integrity. True promotion comes from honesty and integrity. When you have integrity, you allow your true self to be promoted and not a fake you that would eventually lead you to failure in the position you got promoted to. When you truly deserve a promotion, you would be able to get and keep the position while having integrity.

Get a mentor.

One thing that has helped me have integrity is having a personal mentor. By having a personal mentor, it has caused me to constantly have integrity. Let me first say that anyone who you respect and willingly give authority to speak into your life—and you listen to—is your mentor. The problem with many people is that they unconsciously choose the wrong mentor. Choosing the right mentor is key. You must find someone who has the success you want because they will have the wisdom and knowledge it takes to get the success you want. A mentor can be an author from a book you read, a family member, a character in a movie, a music artist, a celebrity, a friend, etc.

Whoever you decide to make your mentor, choose wisely and follow their advice. Having a mentor has affected me by knowing that when no one else is looking, it still feels like someone is watching me because I can hear the voice of correction when I am about to do something wrong. Everyone has two voices that speaks to them, a good voice and a bad voice. By having a mentor, I now recognize the good voice and try to listen to it. Once you have obeyed the good voice for a while, the bad voice begins to dissipate, and you will rarely even hear it.

Let go.

It did take some time for me to get to the place of integrity I'm now at because I used to not like being corrected or yelled at. One of the reasons I didn't like correction was because I would be too scared to lose things that are valuable to me. Responsibilities that had been given to me, I didn't want to lose, so I would lie hoping that I would keep my job, or things I like. That is not living with integrity. If being honest causes you to lose a job, then you probably shouldn't have had it in the first place. Some things you just simply need to let go of, and having integrity will expose them.

Lack of integrity causes financial trouble.

Having integrity will cause people to do business with you and not having integrity will cause people to run away. How can someone trust you if you can't do what you said you were going to do? You will get yourself into a lot of financial trouble when you have a lack of integrity. Lying about paying your bills can cause more bills. Lying about getting stuff done on your job will cause more stress on you because then you must finish the job you said you got done and the new job that was given to you.

A lack of integrity is the reason many people stay broke. If you are always short $50 on your rent every month, and the way you choose to get the $50 is by stealing, you will never have the opportunity to unleash the greatness inside you. When you stretch yourself to come up with ideas to get the amount of money that you need, you will find a way to get it. If you truly care about paying your rent on time, you will find a way to get the money without having to sacrifice integrity. Also, once you have gotten the money you thought you could never get, you then go to a higher level in your life. Getting that extra $50 will become easier, and you will realize that you had a lot more potential inside than you thought.

You will also begin to reach for more, so that you won't ever even have to worry about finances again. If you end up not getting the money you need, then you will go through great pain and loss, but it will be temporary. That pain will cause you to work harder and smarter, so that you will be able to get the finances you need at the right time. Many people see financial hardship as a bad thing, but what they need to realize is that it is simply an opportunity for you to grow. And, for that reason, many people unconsciously remain in poverty. But, integrity is a secret to how people get rich and make it out of poverty.

You need integrity for relationships.

You need to have integrity in order to have real relationships. Whether it be a friend, business partner, a spouse, or whoever, no one wants to be close to someone who doesn't have integrity. No one will be able to trust you if you don't have integrity. A lack of integrity is the reason why many people do not have friends in their lives. With integrity you will gain favor with other people. Although it may be difficult to have integrity—because it will require the real you—it is worth it because integrity will attract the people who really want to be your friends, and you will be able to keep long-lasting relationships.

What to do?

First you must realize the importance of having good character. After making integrity a priority, write out a list of principles that you live by and never break. Then get some friends/leaders around you who also have integrity and will hold you accountable. Having someone to hold you accountable is crucial to your success in this area of life. Always be transparent and not a person who tries to hide things from everyone. Now, being an open person doesn't mean to share everything, but rather to not tell lies about your life; especially, to the people close to you. No one is perfect, so don't be too hard on yourself. Just try your best to keep your word and walk in integrity.

Chapter 9:

Things don't just come to you!

There are nice people, mean people, rich people, poor people, people of all colors, young people, and old people, who die every single day. The world will show you no mercy. You may be nice but, no matter what, you will die physically. That same principle applies to every aspect of life. So, don't grow up thinking that because you're nice, everything will go your way, because it won't.

Things don't just come to you!

Being nice doesn't mean the world will serve you.

Since I was young, I have always been a nice person. I was told then that if you would be nice to others, then life will be nice to you. But, when I became an adult, I found that statement to be false. Some of the nicest people in this world live some of the hardest lives you can ever imagine. Some people become very bitter because of the pains of life. Every day people are mistreated, and there is no way of escaping that while on earth.

Also, I believed that since I prayed, life would be easier for me. Soon I found that to be even more false. Some of the most respected men and women in history, who were/are praying people, lived/are living a very hard and horrific life. These people were being beaten, mistreated, hated, and threatened wherever they went. Being nice is also a recipe for being manipulated. Some people see those who are nice simply as targets to manipulate.

Hard work doesn't always pay off.

I was told growing up that if you work hard, then you will reap a lot. But, I found that to be very false. There are many people on earth who work with every single cell inside of their body, and still get paid very little in return. Much of the time, it is because they are in unfortunate situations.

Some people are born into harsh slavery, poverty, or born homeless. There is no telling why; it may simply be that the world is not nice. People work so hard sometimes and still—even in the midst of giving their all—wonder **can I at least get some reward from it? Shouldn't I get a piece of the cake, as well?** The answer the world gives is no.

A prize to second place may work in elementary school, but in the real world it doesn't. If you lose, you lose; and, you must suffer the consequences. If you have a rent bill that's due for $500 a month, and you have $499 in your account, if the bill collector does not show you mercy, then he has every right to kick you out. It doesn't matter how nice you are, or how hard you tried to come up with the $500. If you don't have that money, then you're out. You must suffer with the consequences the rest of your life and have that on your record.

Life is not a game to play with.

Life is very serious and, although I am a fun person to be around, I take life extremely seriously. It is all we have. If you don't become disciplined in your own, life will make you disciplined. You must become disciplined in order to survive on this earth. A lack of discipline will lead to poverty, depression, frustration from others, and eventually death. Sometimes we must experience pain to make us more disciplined, but you don't have to have this happen to you if you listen to advice. You are only guaranteed one life, so make wise decisions.

The world shows no mercy.

There are nice people, mean people, rich people, poor people, young people, old people, and people of all colors who die daily. The world will show you no mercy. You may be nice but, no matter what, you will physically die. That same principle applies to every aspect of life. So, don't grow up thinking that because you're nice, everything will go your way because it won't.

Make decisions.

You can't flip flop in life; you must learn to make decisions, and stick with them. A good practice for this is whenever you go to a restaurant to eat, make your decision on what to eat quickly, and don't change your mind. Then start to develop the habit of making decisions and sticking with them.

No excuses.

Don't become a complainer because it does you no good. Complaining and giving yourself excuses only weakens you. When you complain, you help whatever situation you are up against automatically win. There is nothing you can do about your past; all you can do is better yourself, and watch your situation become better.

Make things happen!

You need to learn how to make things happen. You need to learn how to stand up for yourself, how to take authority over situations, and how to get what you want. Life will not give you handouts. You may catch a break from time to time, but don't expect it. You need to learn how to go and get it for yourself. Be a hard worker and don't allow bitterness to get to you. As soon as you allow bitterness to get into your heart, life becomes miserable. When you become bitter, you think everyone is against you. When you are bitter, you think the world is against you. You think life sucks; you will resent people; and, you will want to die.

I developed the mentality in sports that I just was going to make it happen. I wouldn't sit around and wait for success to come to me, but that I was going to take it and make it happen. You need to be persistent about getting what you need and want in life. You need to work hard for it. Making things happen must become your nature. If it doesn't become your nature to make things happen, then you are going to live a passive life and may fail at a lot of things.

Get a Coach/Mentor

One way I know how to develop a realistic view of life is coaching. A coach will correct you when you're wrong, help you get what you deserve, ensure to not give you handouts, push you to your limit, and get you in shape to maintain a lifestyle—all while being in a safe-no risk environment. Having a coach or mentor is simulating life without the big risk, so that when real-life challenges come at you, you will be able to overcome.

Your parents can't forever help you.

Mommy and Daddy won't be near you when you get older to help you with any and everything. So, what you're going to have to do is learn how to make things happen. That's what I had to learn when I first moved out and lived on my own. I didn't know hardly anything that I should've known as an adult, but you know what I had to do? Make things happen. If you don't know, then ask... and if no one knows, then just do the best you can. I had to figure out what ever needed to get done and believe that no matter what, I could do it.

To make things happen, you must believe!

You must believe that nothing is impossible. You have to believe that anything is possible because if you don't, then you will quit all the time, and you won't be as successful as you could be. There were many times after I moved out of my parents' house that things seemed impossible, but I had to do what was necessary to get it done. Your mind, when you believe, will find a way to get things done. No matter what the obstacle is, if you don't quit and with enough urgency, your mind will find a way to get something done.

What to do?

Practice being independent and limit what you allow others to do for you. When you are trying something new, do your best to figure it out before asking someone. People who are generally very reliant on others do not get enough brain exercise, so they don't use their brain when it's time to do things that call for brain-power. A way to exercise the brain is to read and surround yourself with intelligent, independent individuals.

Chapter 10:

The Adult Life Never Ends

As an adult, there are too many people counting on you, too many responsibilities, and you have a destiny to be lived out. It's not like when you were a kid where you can just quit and choose a different life route, or get a spanking for a consequence of some sort. If you decide to quit as an adult, then your life falls apart, and if your life falls apart, it then affects those around you.

The adult life never ends

The never-ending adult life:

As an adult, things seem as if they are never ending. You go to work almost every day and, even on your rest day, it seems like you're working. Along with the work, there's also worry and anxiety that tries to overtake you. You have so many things to deal with and so much pressure as an adult. On top of the pressure, you will have to deal with failure because we all make mistakes. Dealing with failure is very tough, and you will want to quit at times—whether that is to just start sleeping all the time, find an addiction, quit your job, or kill yourself. The good news, though, is you're a survivor, and you are greater than life's challenges.

There are too many people counting on you.

As an adult, there are too many people counting on you, too many responsibilities, and you have a destiny to be lived out. It's not like when you were a kid where you could just quit and choose a different life route, or get a spanking for a consequence of some sort. If you decide to quit as an adult, then your life falls apart, and if your life falls apart, it then affects those around you.

If you decide—like a friend of mine—to kill yourself, then your life is over. My friend's one decision caused his family and friends years of pain and grief. If life gets hard, and you choose to quit and kill yourself, you die; you don't have another chance to make it up. That's not just the result of choosing to kill yourself, but it is also quitting in any area of life.

If you are a manager at a good job, and you decide to quit, that is your money. You will not be getting paid anymore until you find a new job. You won't be able to eat, and most likely that job will not want you back. If you quit on your job and don't have any money, then your own family won't be able to survive. If you quit on your marriage, then your kids will grow up with extra issues. Life is very serious, so you can't just quit because things are hard; you must press through.

Build stamina.

Learn to not quit and to have the stamina to keep going. I think one of the best things someone young can do is a sport that takes stamina, such as cross-country, basketball, etc. It is a realistic picture of life because, in life, you get short breaks—and they are far and few.

Winners don't quit.

Always remember that there is hope for you, there is hope for your student, there is hope for your protégé, there is hope for your client, there is hope for your parent, and there is hope for your child. Never give up on yourself, or anyone that you have been chosen to be an influence to. People grow. Just like a seed needs time to grow into a beautiful plant, so do you and every other person.

There is a process to building a successful, mature adult. I didn't become who I am today overnight. There have been many times since I started my journey that I have failed. But there is one significant difference between a winner and a loser; winners do not quit. You can never win if you quit. Just because you fail doesn't mean that you are not on the right track. The reason that so many people consider their lives miserable is because they quit. Always remember that you can never fail if you never quit.

Think about the end result.

When you feel like giving up, just think about the end from the beginning. Think about the good end result of continuing and working hard, and also think about the bad result of quitting. Whenever you quit, you must start all over; it is terrible. When I quit football the first time and got back in it the second time, it took me a long time to even get nearly as good as I was previously... even though I was older.

Handling failure.

People quit because they don't know how to handle failure. Also, people think that because they failed that they were doing something wrong. Failure is simply a situation that occurs to help you improve who you are and your skill. If you have the right attitude and perspective towards failure, you will notice that it is possible to never fail in life. True failure only occurs when you give up. I'm not saying that failure does not hurt, but next time you encounter failure, see it as an opportunity instead of an end result. Learn from your failure, get back up, grow from it, and keep moving forward stronger than you were before.

Never stop dreaming.

I want to encourage you today to not quit on your dreams or visions. Do you have a vision or a dream to do something big? Don't quit on it, make it happen. Your dreams and visions will fuel you to continue through life. Without dreams and visions, it will be easy to quit because there's nothing to live for. I believe that if you don't have a dream or a vision that you are working towards, then you are living a meaningless life. What have you always wanted to achieve or do? I hope that through reading this book you will choose to reawaken the dream inside you and begin to live a life of passion.

Take a break.

A great solution for feeling exhausted or burnt out is to simply take a break. Nobody is superman, so at some point you will get tired. When that happens, just take a break. You do not have to quit everything in order to feel rested. You can take a 15-minute nap, eat a meal, take a day off, or go on a vacation. However long you need to rest, make it happen; just don't quit.

Your decisions matter.

You must make good decisions because it not only affects you and the people around you, but it also affects generations to come. Many people today are struggling and feeling trapped in life simply because of a poor decision one of their ancestors made. Your decisions impact more people and more powerfully than you could imagine. Many people just go through life thinking that there is nothing really to live for and hoping their kids become better than they did. But what do you really expect of your kids, if you are setting a poor example for them to follow?

You are the first example your kids see, and they are most likely to follow you more than anyone else. Also, the people around you are watching you, whether you want to believe it or not. Most people are followers and are looking for a person to follow. When you are living a purposeful life, you help bring the people around you into their purpose simply by leading by example. When you are living a stagnant life, you will unconsciously bring others around you down and keep them living either a stagnant or destructive life as well. Remember that each person knows someone else, so how you impact one person will impact another person. Don't believe the lies that say you can't make a difference because you have the power inside you to change the world. You are on this earth for a reason; find out what that reason is and pursue it!

Get up!

If you have quit in life, you can always get up. People tell me to be realistic and to live in reality until they begin seeing results. The reality is that you need to be believing the unseen truth of today, so that you will manifest your dreams and visions tomorrow. So, no matter where you are in life, get up because you are a champion; that's who you are on the inside. You can make it to the end, and you can overcome obstacles. You must live with faith and believe that you can overcome any obstacle. You will be in situations that seem impossible, but don't let it intimidate you. Know that you are a champion, you are a conqueror, and you are victorious.

What to do?

- Build stamina by doing endurance workouts.

- Also, read more books so that your brain remains active.
- Singing will also help you stay positive and keep you in good energy throughout the day.
- While going throughout your day, make upcoming plans and write down goals.
- Also, take a few minutes to clean each day instead of sitting doing nothing; it will help build stamina.

Do those five things, and you will notice your days are becoming less strenuous.

"If you don't quit, you will win."

About the Author

Kenneth Smith Jr is originally from New Orleans and was born in 1995. He and his family were greatly impacted by Hurricane Katrina in 2005 which made them move to Dallas, Texas. He learned quickly to never over value material possessions so he made living for a purpose his main priority in life.

Instead of getting wrapped up in the party scene in high school, Kenneth chose to spend those years and after dedicated to impacting others. He was a part of plenty of groups and organizations to reach the homeless, speak to schools, and find creative ways to help someone hurting. Even on his downtime, he would go with his friends to reach others.

After High School, Kenneth had a tough time finding out what he wanted to do in life and struggled as a young adult. He was confused because he felt since he was trying to help people that everything else would be taken care of.

At 18, Kenneth was far behind when it came to maturity. He learned quickly that their is a lot more to life than helping others and just because you are nice does not mean life will be nice to you. Through hard work and the help of a mentor, Kenneth started to see the light at the end of the tunnel.

He has now worked himself to being a top seller in his company, a published author, and investor. He now is passionate about helping people get on their two feet. He used to simply want to feed the poor but now he believes that the best thing you can give to someone is information to transform their life.

Kenneth is on a mission to help people under 18 and over 18 to get established in life. "Give a man a fish and you'll feed him for a day, but if you teach him how to fish, you feed him for a lifetime".